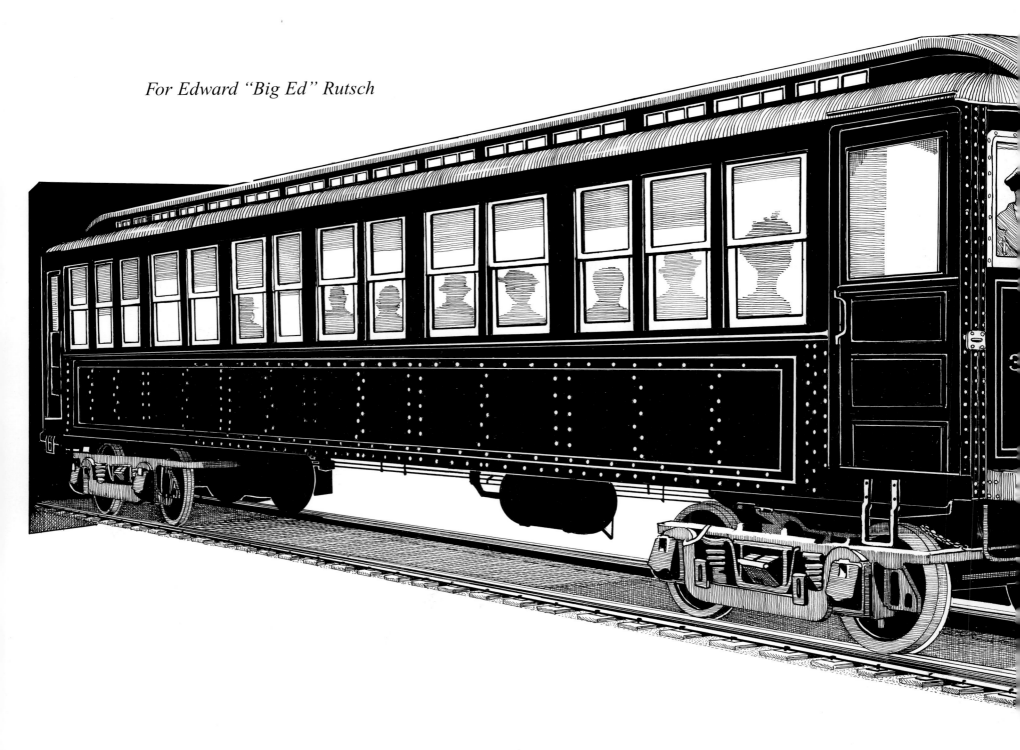

For Edward "Big Ed" Rutsch

David Weitzman

A SUBWAY FOR NEW YORK

Farrar, Straus and Giroux / New York

New York in 1900, with a population of 3.4 million people, was the second-largest city in the world after London. Buildings were getting so tall—over twenty stories—that people worried that the narrow island of Manhattan might tip over into the river.

New York's docks attracted ships from distant ports with goods for a growing nation and immigrants seeking a new life. Almost a million immigrants came through New York in 1900 alone, mostly from southern and eastern Europe and the Middle East. One out of every three children in New York's schools had immigrant parents. And millions more would come in the next few years. In a single lifetime the population of New York tripled.

Every day tens of thousands of workers crossed the bridges into Manhattan from the surrounding boroughs, adding to the congestion. It could take two hours or more to get from one end of the island to the other. There had to be a better way to get around.

The answer was to build a transit system to move people swiftly under the city streets. London opened the world's first subway in 1863. Other European cities followed suit: Budapest and Glasgow (1896), Paris (1900), Berlin (1902). After three years of construction, Boston opened America's first subway in 1898, but the system envisioned by planners in New York would be the most ambitious to date.

The streets were jammed helter-skelter with pedestrians, pushcarts, horse-drawn wagons and buggies, streetcars, bicycles, even a few horseless carriages. From overhead came the constant clatter of elevated trains pulled by steam locomotives that belched thick black smoke and rained ashes, fiery cinders, scalding water, and sparks down onto the streets below

On February 21, 1900, Contract No. 1 for building and operating the subway was signed, and new initials entered New Yorkers' vocabulary—IRT, the Interborough Rapid Transit. But not all New Yorkers saw the wisdom of a subway. One critic scoffed, "New York people will never go into a hole in the ground to ride. Preposterous!"

Still, plans for the subway moved forward, and a network of routes was selected. On the west side of Manhattan, the subway would run between the northern and southern ends of the island, primarily beneath Broadway, the most direct path. This would be the first portion of the subway to open, four and a half years later.

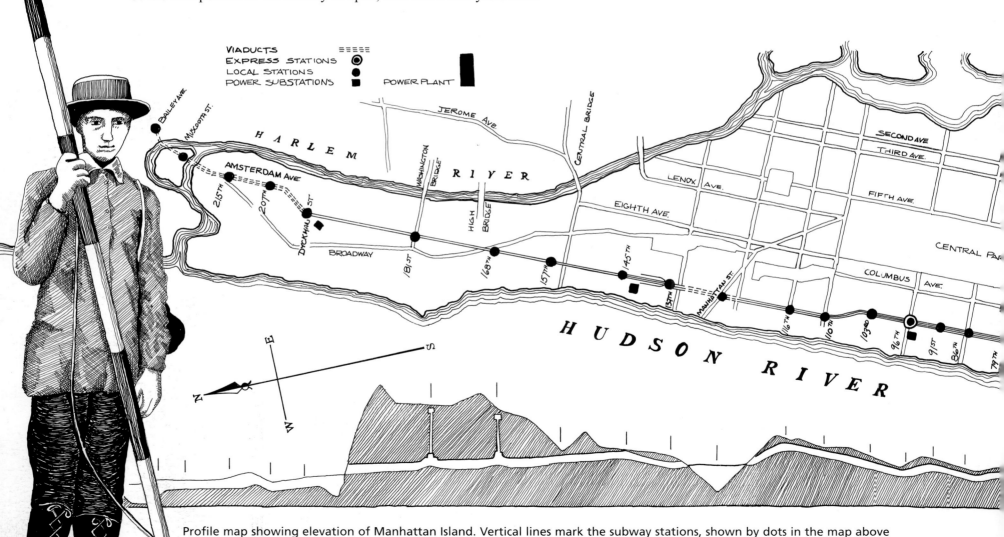

Profile map showing elevation of Manhattan Island. Vertical lines mark the subway stations, shown by dots in the map above

Manhattan has many peaks and valleys. To keep the subway level and safe under the hills of upper Manhattan, engineers planned a tunnel over two miles long. At 168th Street and 181st Street the stations were going to be so deep that elevators would be needed to get riders to and from the platform. At Manhattan Street—now 125th Street—the tracks would emerge from the tunnel and cross a 2,174-foot steel arch.

With today's crowded Manhattan in mind, it's hard to imagine that the northern end of the line would run through little villages, farms, farmers' markets, and fields of cabbage.

Map of Manhattan showing the planned IRT subway route along Broadway. In 1904, the first train ran from City Hall to 145th Street

Before subway building could begin, workers had to relocate the web of sewers, water and gas mains, steam pipes, telegraph and electric lines, and streetcar cables just under the surface of the streets. Because sewers in Manhattan run east and west to the Hudson and East rivers, the subway excavation required moving and replacing almost every sewer line in the city!

There were no maps to show what was under the streets. What was discovered was a jumble of pipes and cables that first had to be sorted out, labeled, and then carefully moved. Gas mains required the greatest care. To prevent underground explosions, the gas mains were "killed" and new lines run temporarily aboveground. Some mains were laid along the curb; others were carried on raised scaffolding above the sidewalk.

Craftsmen—mostly immigrants—built new sewer lines of brick and concrete, using wooden forms to hold up the brick until the mortar set

At the request of a civil rights leader, the transit company agreed to hire five hundred African Americans to help build the subway. There are no records of the number actually hired, but we do know that African Americans were involved in many aspects of the construction work

Subway construction began on March 24, 1900. First, the paving stones and pavement were taken up. Horse-drawn plows broke up the compacted earth. Then, with picks and shovels, thousands of workers scraped, dug, and blasted miles of open trenches and tunnels entirely by hand—millions of wheelbarrow- and wagonloads of soil, sand, and rock.

Working on one side of the street at a time, crews dug down six to eight feet and immediately constructed above themselves a temporary roadway and sidewalk of heavy timbers and planks. Then work could continue underground while life continued on the streets above. This way of building subways is called "cut-and-cover."

Digging into the ground took the workers into the past: they unearthed huge mastodon bones, a Dutch merchant ship that caught fire and sank in 1614 and had since been covered with landfill, the hollowed-out pine logs of the city's first water supply system. Workers even cut into the remains of an earlier experimental pneumatic subway, built in secret in 1870

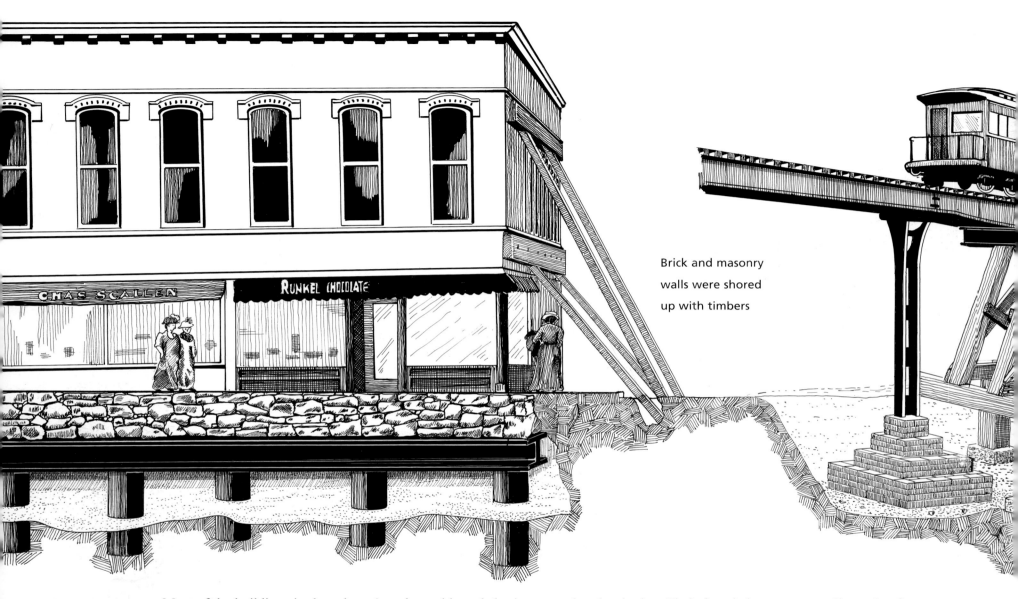

Brick and masonry
walls were shored
up with timbers

Most of the buildings in the subway's path would need shoring up and underpinning. Their foundations were usually made of loose stone, rubble, or brick laid in trenches. Any disturbance of the soil under the foundation could—and sometimes did—result in the entire building tumbling down into a heap. Before the subway was begun, every building along the route was photographed. If a property owner later claimed damages from the builders, a record existed clearly showing if the damage was already there or occurred after the start of construction.

One way of underpinning foundations and buildings was with steel beams supported by pipes driven down to rock. Where workers encountered the brick footing supporting the columns of elevated-railroad structures, temporary timber A-frames were constructed. Eventually, the columns would stand on the concrete roof of the completed subway.

Streets and streetcar tracks had to be shored up so traffic was not interrupted while the subway building went on below

As soon as workmen finished digging the trench, the work of building the subway speedily followed. First, workers poured a four-inch-thick concrete foundation over the entire floor of the trench (1). Then they covered the foundation with layers of felt mopped with hot asphalt to keep water from seeping up through the floor (2). Terra-cotta duct banks (3) were laid along both edges of the floor to form side walls. Later, workers would thread through them the electric cables for running the trains, controlling the many switches and signals, and lighting the stations. These ducts would also carry the heavy cables bringing power from the subway's powerhouse. The outside of the duct banks were also sealed with felt and asphalt.

Rows of cut stone footings (4) set five feet apart supported the steel I-beam frames (5) that formed the skeleton of the tunnel. Once the framework was erected, a second layer of concrete (6) was poured all around the stone footings and the bases of the outside I beams, leaving spaces between the rows for laying the tracks. Where there would be stations, the concrete was strengthened with $1\frac{1}{8}$-inch reinforcing rods (7).

Waterproofing the floor, walls, and eventually the roof kept water out but resulted in an unforeseen problem—it also kept heat in. All the friction of brake shoes on wheels and wheels on rails, the hundreds of electric motors operating at one time, the thousands of incandescent lights, and the body heat of thousands of passengers could not escape, and the tunnels became intolerably hot. Later, ventilation shafts and sidewalk grates would be added along the line

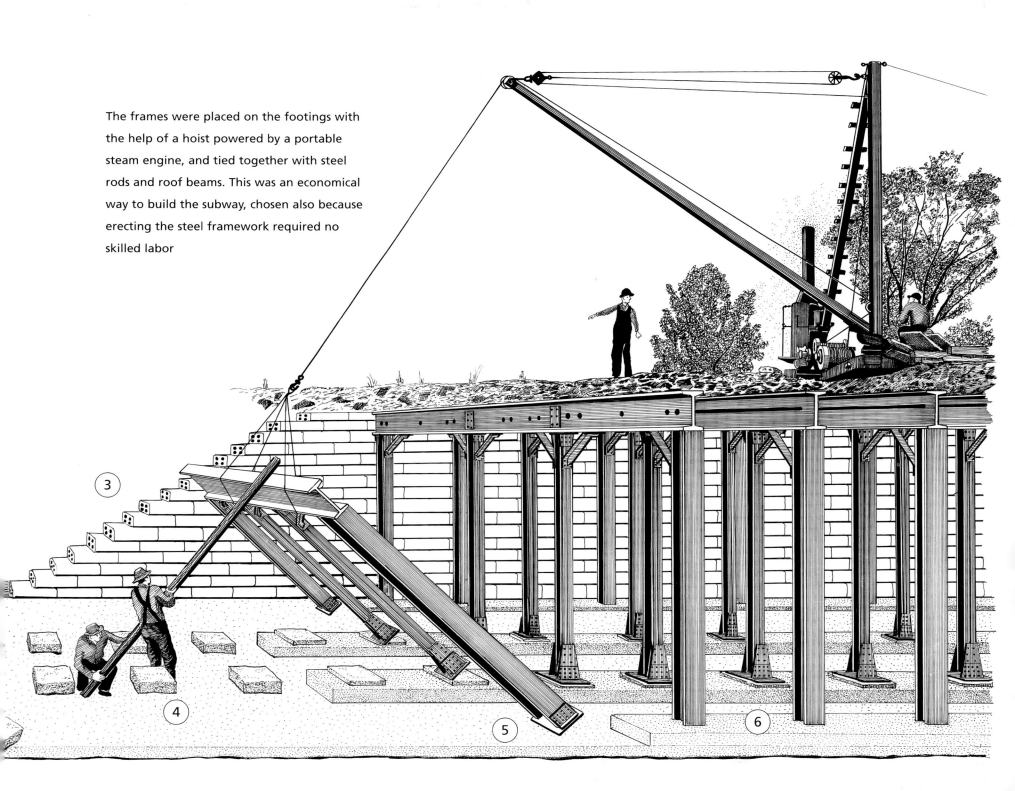

The frames were placed on the footings with the help of a hoist powered by a portable steam engine, and tied together with steel rods and roof beams. This was an economical way to build the subway, chosen also because erecting the steel framework required no skilled labor

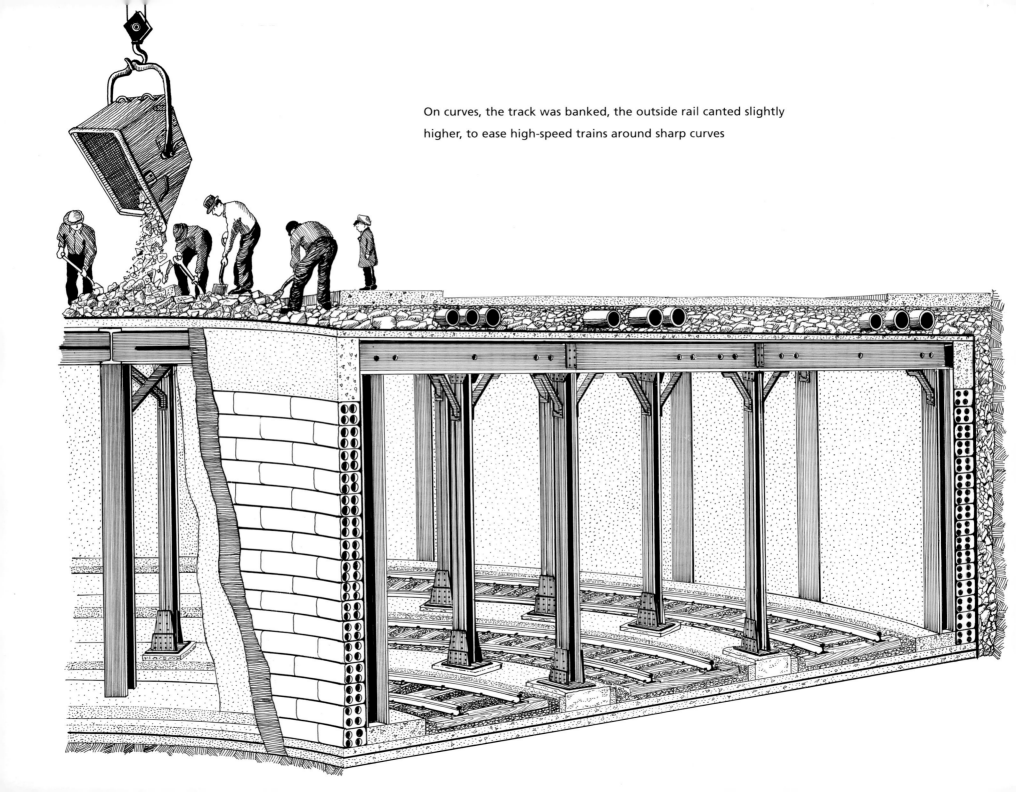

On curves, the track was banked, the outside rail canted slightly higher, to ease high-speed trains around sharp curves

Now, with the framework in place, the concrete walls and roof could be poured between the steel beams. All the pipes and wires that had been moved before the digging began were replaced and covered with soil and rock. And, with the rebuilding of sidewalks and streets, the city began to look normal once again.

Below, crews were now laying track on which the trains would run. Yellow-pine ties were spaced out on a cushion of crushed rock. The ties had been soaked in creosote to prevent them from rotting. Track workers then laid the rails and fastened them down with spikes. Finally, more crushed rock was tamped down between the ties.

At stations, the track layout was different. Rails were laid on short creosote-soaked blocks of wood, which were embedded in concrete. The concrete was sloped to form a trough down the center with drains so that the tracks could be hosed down.

By now the Boston subway had been running long enough to teach New York's subway engineers some important lessons. Ordinary steel was fine for straight track, but not for curves. All the grinding, grating, and shrieking that subway riders suffer as trains lurch around tight curves comes from the wheel flanges scraping against the outside rail. Ordinary steel rails in the Boston subway lasted only sixty days. But in the New York subway, special rails of steel alloyed with manganese were used for curves and switches and lasted over six years.

Anyone who has ridden at the front of the train knows that the tracks are not level, but rise and fall. Engineers tried to keep the subway as close to the surface as possible. But sometimes the tunnel had to descend below the deep foundations of buildings before climbing closer to the surface to make excavation easier and stations more accessible to the street. The tracks also climb slightly at the approach to each station, slowing the high-speed trains to a smoother braking and stop. At the other end of the station the tracks descend, helping the trains to accelerate

Cut-and-cover was possible where the trench was close to the surface and the walls of the trench would stand up. But when the subway had to go deep or through soft sand and mud, tunneling was required. About a quarter of the first subway required tunneling. This was the most dangerous work of all, and the men who did this work were called "sandhogs."

One major problem sandhogs encountered was water. Because Manhattan is almost at sea level, crews were always digging into clay, sand saturated with water, or an underground spring that suddenly flooded the tunnel. Another danger was loose rock that crashed in on the sandhogs when they tried to dig. Under these conditions, work could continue only when using a shield, a steel-and-cast-iron cylinder that protected the workers.

If water began seeping into the tunnel, compressed air was pumped in until the pressure was high enough to counter the pressure behind the water and stop the flow. Sandhogs called this "working in air," and it meant they were working at pressures two or three times what their bodies were used to. They had to take frequent rests at normal air pressure. Whenever they entered or left the tunnel, the sandhogs had to spend time in the air lock while the pressure was gradually raised or lowered to allow their bodies to adjust.

Working in air was dangerous. The effects of compression and decompression on humans were not well understood in those days. If decompression went too fast, air bubbles formed in the blood, causing "the bends." Many workers suffered severe pain in their joints, paralysis, permanent crippling, and even death before the correct times for decompression were worked out.

The air around us presses in on our bodies at about fifteen pounds per square inch, one atmosphere. Sandhogs sometimes had to work at three atmospheres, their bodies under some forty-five pounds of pressure—the maximum humans can tolerate. At two atmospheres, sandhogs worked three hours, took a three-hour rest at atmospheric pressure, then worked three more hours. At three atmospheres, a four-hour rest was required

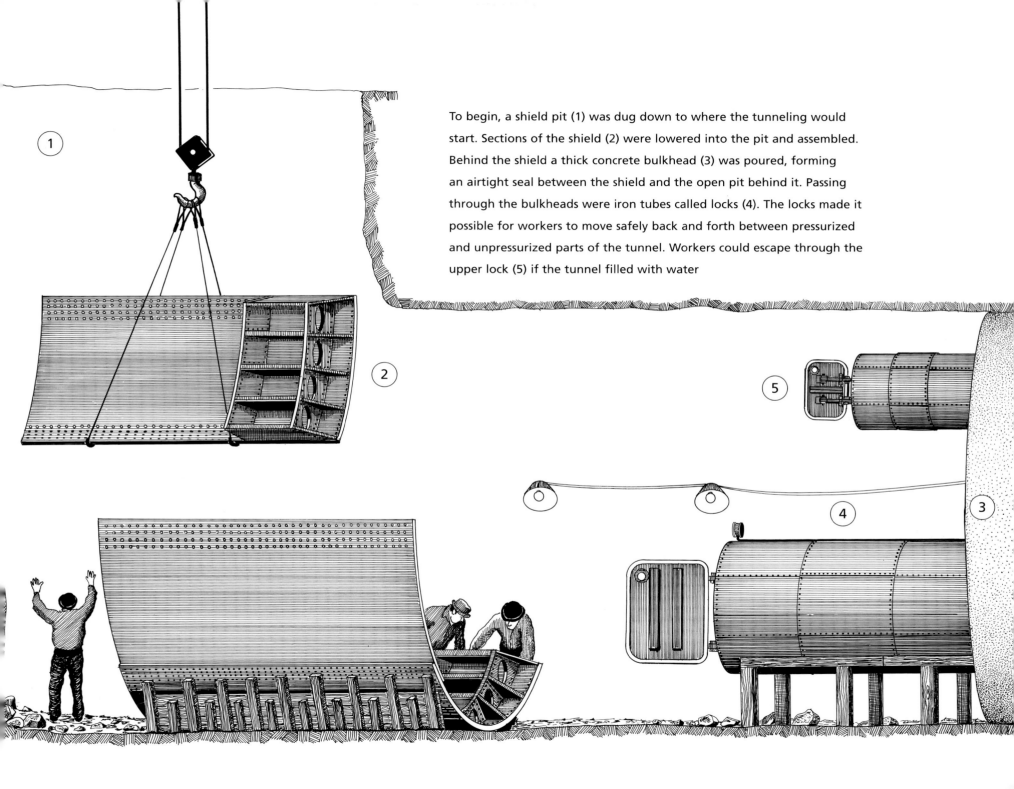

To begin, a shield pit (1) was dug down to where the tunneling would start. Sections of the shield (2) were lowered into the pit and assembled. Behind the shield a thick concrete bulkhead (3) was poured, forming an airtight seal between the shield and the open pit behind it. Passing through the bulkheads were iron tubes called locks (4). The locks made it possible for workers to move safely back and forth between pressurized and unpressurized parts of the tunnel. Workers could escape through the upper lock (5) if the tunnel filled with water

The massive shield was made of 2¹⁄₈-inch-thick steel plate and weighed almost two hundred tons. It was designed to withstand the crushing forces of the earth and rock around it and also to move forward under tremendous pressure.

The front of the shield formed a sharp cutting edge and a hood (1) to protect the drillers from falling rocks. At the back were compressed-air-powered rams (2), which exerted over six million pounds of force. After the sandhogs had cleared a space in front of the shield, the rams extended (3) and pushed the entire shield forward.

Each time the shield moved forward, a space (4) was left behind just wide enough for another ring of cast iron (5). These

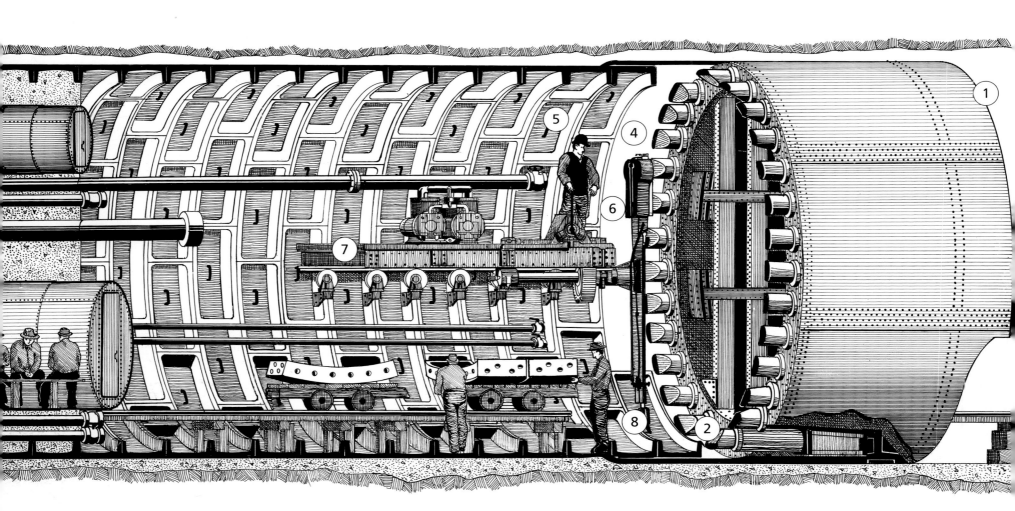

rings became the permanent tunnel. Each segment weighed over a ton, but was easily put in place by an erector arm (6) mounted on a carriage (7). The carriage followed the shield on wheels. The erector arm rotated like the big hand of a clock, picking up each segment and spinning it around into position. A piston on the end of the arm (8) then extended, pushing the segment neatly into place. Finally, sandhogs bolted the sections together with a wrench weighing seventy-five pounds.

Again, the rams were extended out in the shove position, pushing against the ring just erected behind the shield. And when the rams were retracted, a new ring was put into the space left behind.

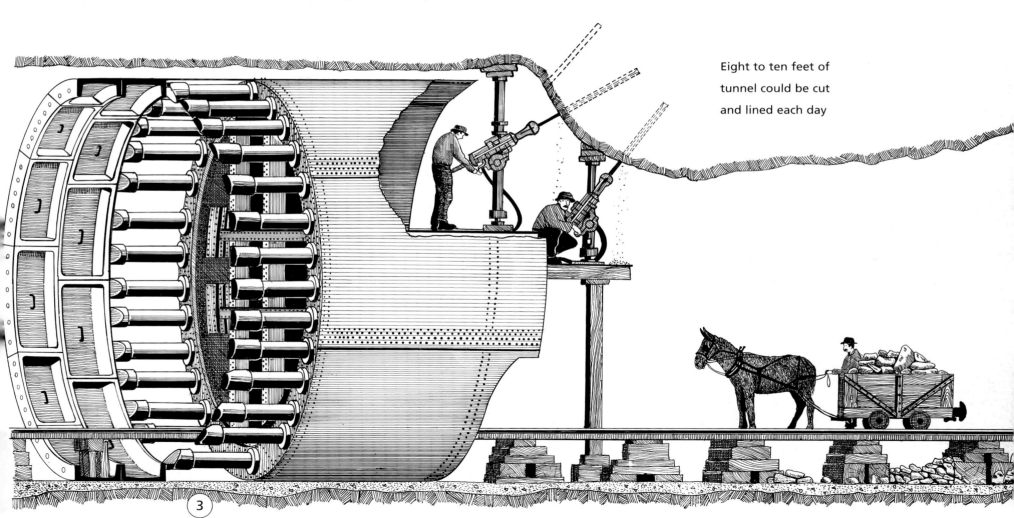

Eight to ten feet of tunnel could be cut and lined each day

Wherever the sandhogs ran into hard rock and huge boulders, they blasted their way through. Workers labored through the night drilling holes into which they would place powerful explosives that shattered the rock. The hard rock quickly dulled the tools, which required sharpening after about a foot of drilling. Drillers' helpers were kept busy collecting the dull tools and hauling them to a hoist. The hoist lifted them up to wagons that were waiting to take them to the drill shop and bring them back straightened and sharpened.

By early morning the holes were ready to receive the explosives. The drillers placed sticks of dynamite into each hole, attached blasting caps, and ran wires back to the blasting box, which ignited the charges with an electric current. Heavy blasting mats covered the walls to keep rock from flying back into the tunnel.

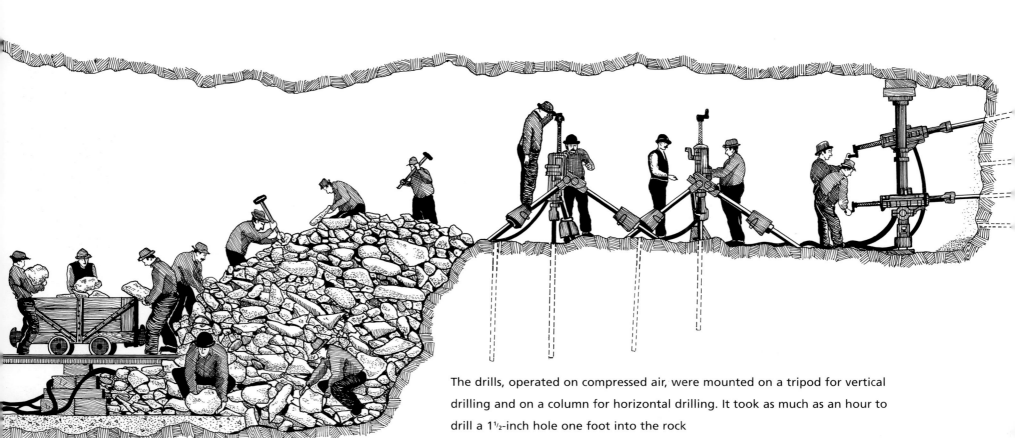

The drills, operated on compressed air, were mounted on a tripod for vertical drilling and on a column for horizontal drilling. It took as much as an hour to drill a 1½-inch hole one foot into the rock

When it was time to blast, a steam whistle sounded three times: a five-minute warning, a three-minute warning, and a one-minute warning. The workers scrambled back to the safety of the shield. The foreman gave the final warning to make sure everyone was clear. Then there was a deafening roar followed by the clatter of tumbling rocks, and a dense, swirling cloud of dust that filled the tunnel and the workers' lungs.

The day gang moved in to clear away the spoil: the blasted rock. By evening it was removed, in time for the drillers to begin again.

The rocks and boulders were loaded into skips, which were then hauled by mules to the shaft, where a hoist lifted them to the surface and the waiting wagons. Most of the rock was crushed to make concrete

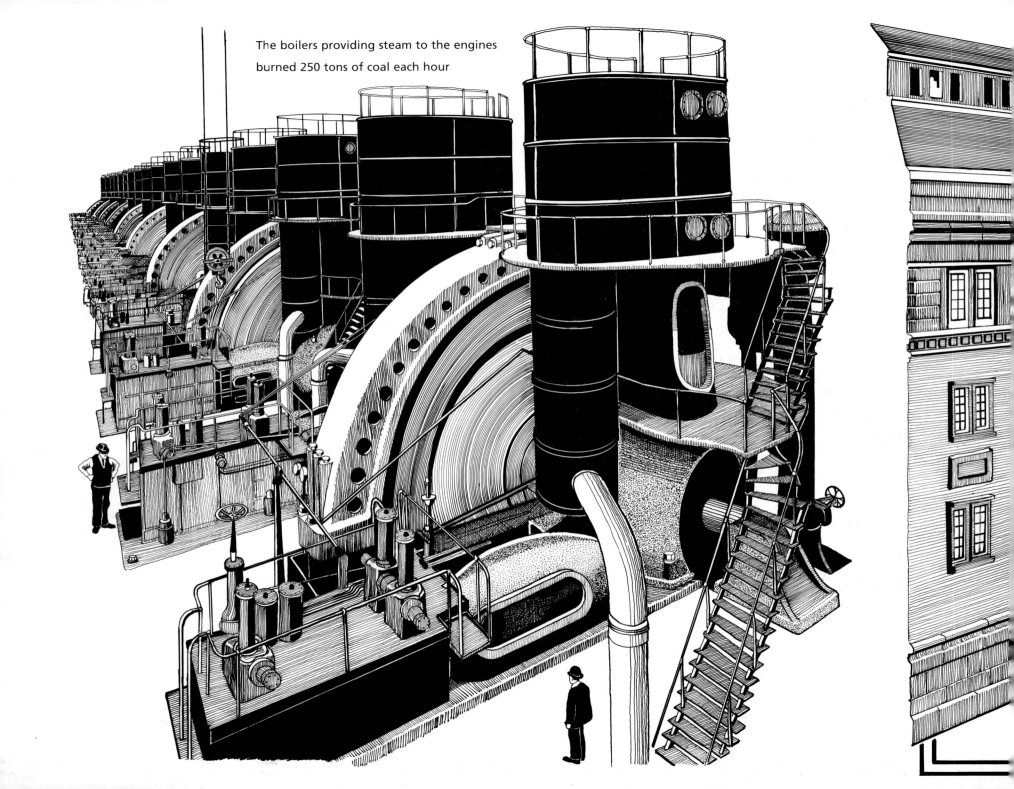

The boilers providing steam to the engines burned 250 tons of coal each hour

As thousands of workers built the subway, others were constructing the power system that would generate electricity to run the trains and light the stations—a powerhouse and eight substations.

The massive IRT powerhouse between 58th and 59th streets on the Hudson River was designed to generate more electricity than any electrical plant ever built. Ten steam engines, five stories tall, turning massive dynamos generated enough electricity to run what was an underground city.

The riverside was a necessary site. River water passed through fish traps into tunnels that carried it to reservoirs feeding the boilers. Coal arrived on long strings of barges and was carried by conveyor belts from the wharf through tunnels to bunkers storing 18,000 tons.

Before it could be used to run trains, the electricity from the generators had to be distributed to the eight substations along the subway line. Cables carried the current from the powerhouse to the subway at 58th and Broadway. And here they were fed through the duct banks connecting all the stations and the electric substations along the line.

The powerhouse exterior was as impressive as what it contained. It was built of cream-colored brick on a cut-granite base, with decorations of marble and terra-cotta. And towering above were six red brick chimneys, each 162 feet tall

11,000 volts AC

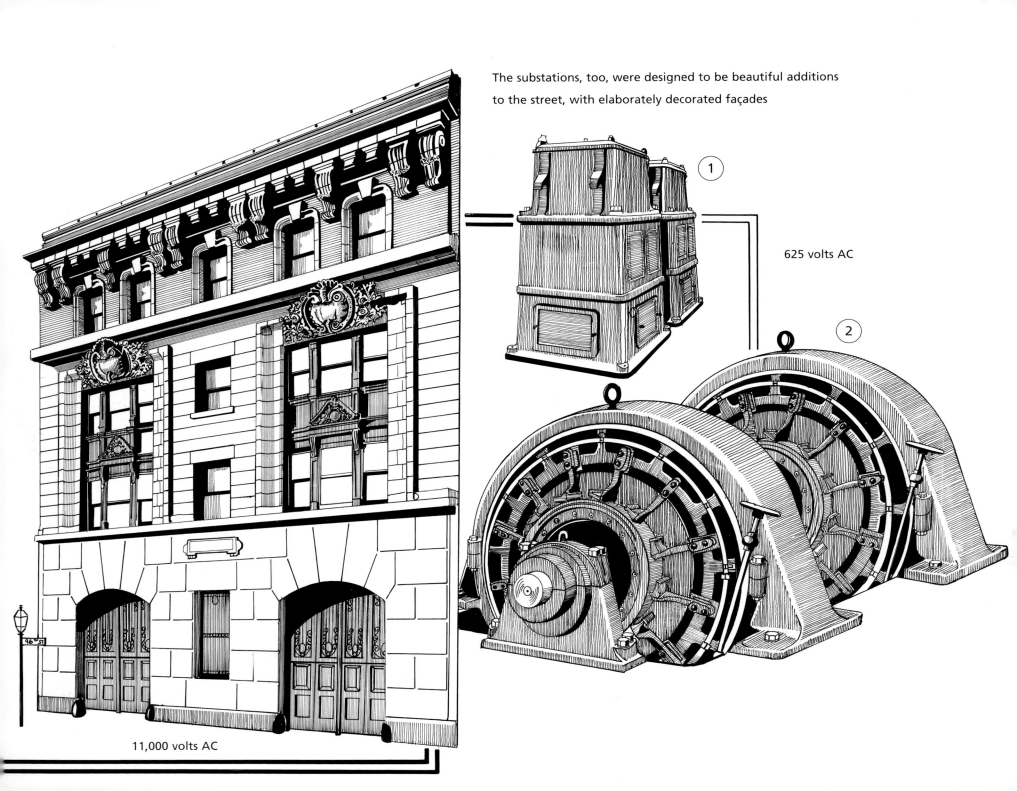

The substations, too, were designed to be beautiful additions to the street, with elaborately decorated façades

1

625 volts AC

2

11,000 volts AC

The eight substations converted the electricity generated at the powerhouse into what was needed to run the trains. At the substation the 11,000 volts AC (alternating current) went first through transformers (1) that reduced the voltage to 625 volts. This was the voltage required to run the electric motors on the cars. But the motors ran on DC (direct current), and so the electricity also had to go through a converter (2). From the converter the direct current was sent to the contact, or third, rail (3), controlled by large knife switches (4) on a feeder board. Each substation supplied power to a portion of the system, shown on a map (5) above the switches. A trainmaster sat at a central board that showed him the whole system. He could call for more or less power from each substation, depending on the number of trains running at one time.

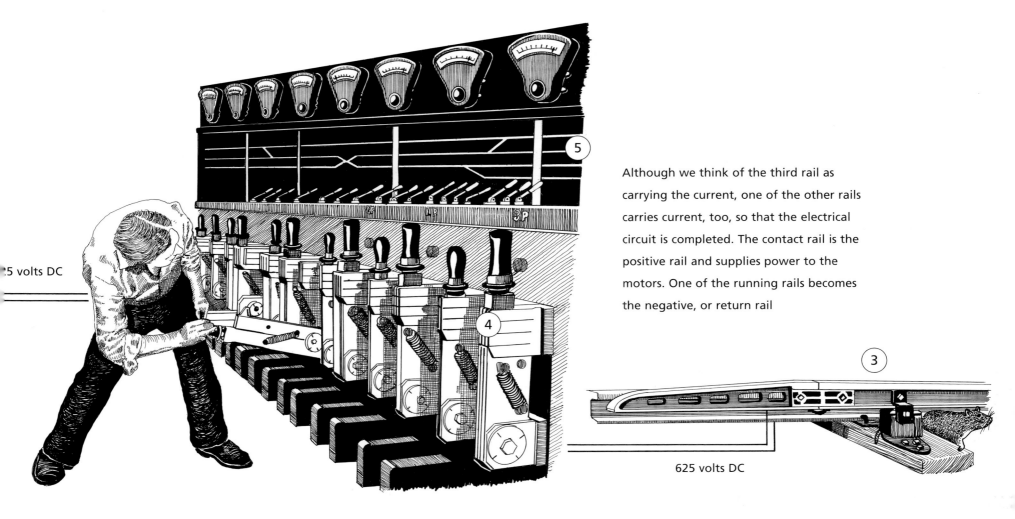

Although we think of the third rail as carrying the current, one of the other rails carries current, too, so that the electrical circuit is completed. The contact rail is the positive rail and supplies power to the motors. One of the running rails becomes the negative, or return rail

5 volts DC

625 volts DC

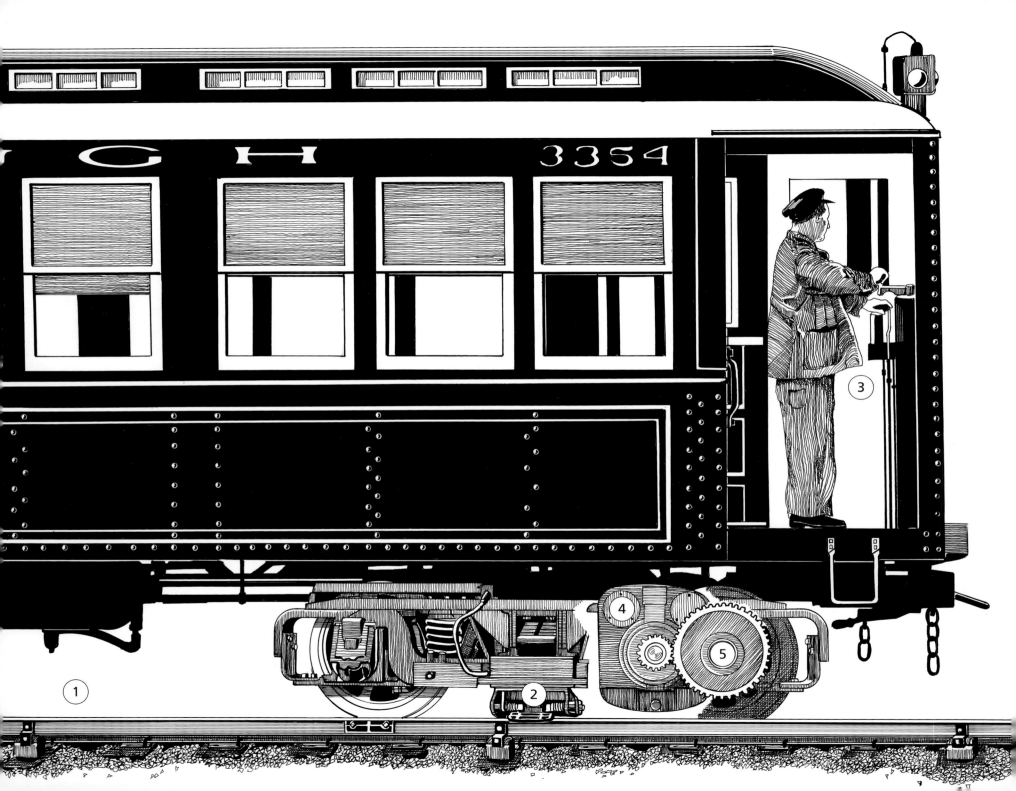

The electrical current in the contact rail (1) traveled to the motor through contact shoes (2) that slid along the top of the third rail, held down by springs.

From the contact shoes, the electricity went to the controller (3) in the motorman's cab at the front of the train. The front car was not a locomotive that pulled the whole train. Instead, when the motorman moved the control handle to start the train, he sent electricity to motors (4) on his and other cars. The cutaway drawing shows how the motor was geared to the axle (5).

Not all the cars had motors. The cars were coupled together in pairs of one motor car and one trail car. When these were put together into a train, it was always possible to add or remove two cars at either end and still have a motor car at the front of the train.

Running the train required only two controls. The motorman applied and released the air brakes with his right hand. His left hand was on the control handle, in the center of which was a knob called the "deadman's control." If the motorman's left hand came off that knob for any reason while the train was moving, the train was brought to an emergency stop.

New Yorkers rode in stronger, safer cars than on any electric railway in the world, the first to be made entirely of steel. Sliding doors replaced the old gates. Passengers sat on comfortable seats of woven rattan. The floors were of maple, the walls of mahogany, and standing passengers steadied themselves by holding overhead leather straps (and forever after becoming known as "straphangers").

Subway trains traveled much faster than elevated trains. The average speed of express trains, including stops, was twenty-five miles per hour, and they reached a maximum speed of forty-five miles per hour. Think about how different this was—and still is—from traffic up on the streets

New York's new subway would be the most efficient in the world, and the first to have separate tracks for express trains—the two center tracks. Express trains made the run between the Brooklyn Bridge and 96th Street stations in just sixteen minutes, with only three stops in between. Local trains covered the same distance in twenty-six minutes. Of course, rush-hour trips, with more trains running, took a little longer.

During the first two months of the subway's operation, more than sixteen million tickets were sold for a nickel a ride. During the first year, there were over a hundred million fares

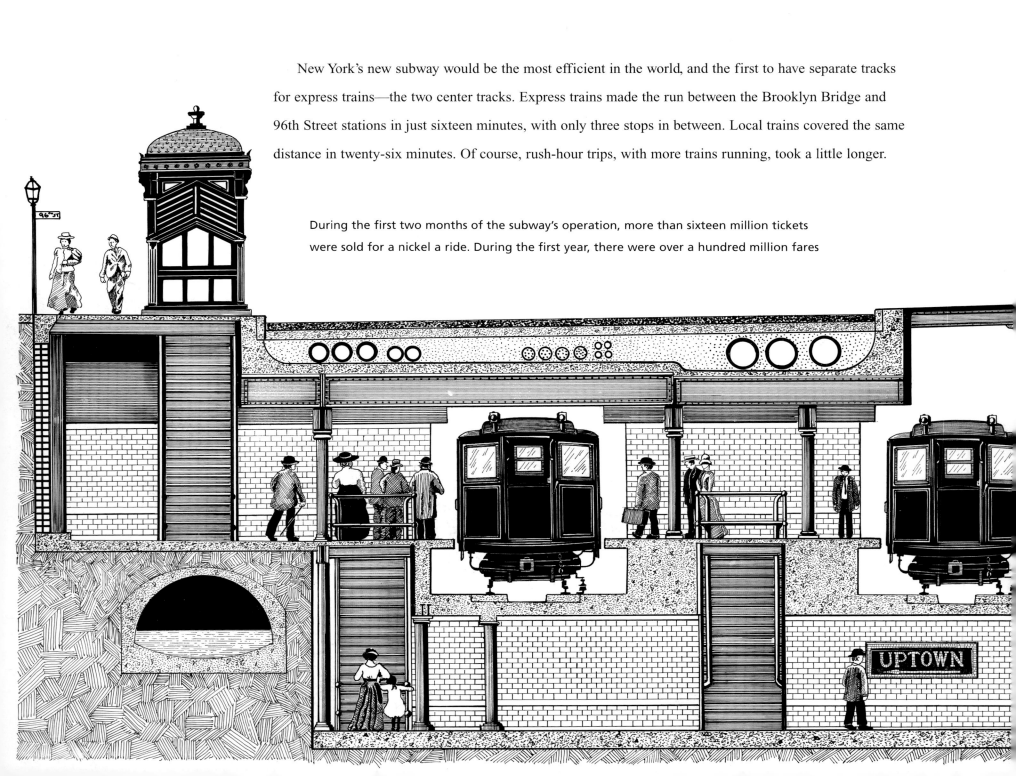

Much of the efficiency came from the carefully considered design of the stations and the cars, which could accommodate sixty thousand people an hour. As shown in this cross section of the station at 96th Street and Broadway, island platforms enabled passengers to transfer between local and express trains just by stepping across the platform. Passageways under the tracks at many stations allowed crowds access to uptown and downtown service from all street entrances. All the stations were brightly illuminated with electric light.

DOWNTOWN

Astor Place (named for John Jacob Astor, who made his fortune in beaver pelts), terra-cotta panel

Brooklyn Bridge, faience panel

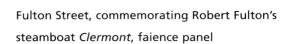

Fulton Street, commemorating Robert Fulton's steamboat *Clermont*, faience panel

Entrance and exit kiosk at Astor Place, based on a Hungarian interpretation of ancient Persian and Turkish summerhouses, cast iron

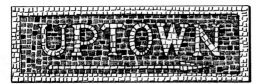

Ceramic-tile mosaic panels

The budget for the first subway included $500,000 to be spent on decorating the new stations. According to Contract No. 1, the subway stations were to be "a great public work" to be designed "with a view to the beauty of their appearance as well as their efficiency."

Architects set out to make the unfamiliar space more appealing and comfortable, at the same time making each station distinctive in color and design so that passengers could easily recognize their stop. This was an especially important consideration for immigrant passengers who did not read English.

The subway's designers used two new architectural materials—reinforced concrete to form the intricate arches of the City Hall station, and architectural terra-cotta, molded clay glazed with bright colors and baked in a kiln. They also created decorations of ceramic tile, glazed brick, marble, and faience, a glazed pottery.

Canal Street, depicting the Stone Bridge Tavern and the stone bridge on Broadway that crossed the canal, mosaic panel

City Hall, glazed brick arches

The first portion of the IRT subway opened on October 27, 1904, to great fanfare. It had taken many years to plan and over four years to build. Trains sped passengers from City Hall in lower Manhattan to 145th Street and Broadway in a fraction of the time it would take on the city streets. On that first day 150,000 New Yorkers lined up at the stations to ride.

And very soon the city's first subway was almost overwhelmed by passengers. Work continued in order to expand service to new stations and routes as soon as possible. In 1914 lines with a capacity of 400,000 passengers a day were actually carrying 1.2 million passengers. By 1915 the subway had expanded to connect four of the city's five boroughs. While almost entirely underground in Manhattan, trains ran underground, on elevated tracks, in open trenches, and at ground level through Brooklyn, Queens, and the Bronx.

Today the subway is the world's longest, with 722 miles of track along 244 miles of routes. Over a billion riders each year pay up to two dollars a trip. "Beneath the sidewalks of New York," it's been said, "the subways have created a second city [and] the New Yorker could live a rather rounded life without once venturing into the street."

Over one hundred years after it opened, the subway remains the fastest and most efficient way to get around New York City.

ACKNOWLEDGMENTS

My special thanks go to the staff of the New York Transit Museum, particularly Junnko Tozaki and archivist Miriam K. Tierney, who answered my many queries with images and documents from the museum's collections.

I was able to look through thousands of historical photographs in just two days, thanks to the efficiency and cooperation of the staff of the New-York Historical Society's Department of Prints, Photographs, and Architectural Collections. Its photographs enabled me to reconstruct the smallest details of the workers' lives, the subway building, and the ongoing change in the city landscape.

My researcher in New York, Elizabeth Frenchman, came up with oral histories and first-person accounts of the sandhogs to enrich and enliven their story and mine.

Gerry Weinstein somehow managed to find in his private collection images I was unable to locate anywhere else, often sending me things I needed before I knew I needed them. And to Peter Derrick of the Bronx Historical Society my appreciation for his astute comments, suggestions, and corrections.

The quote on the preceding page comes from a reprint of *The WPA Guide to New York City* (New York: The New Press, 1995), p. 402.

SUGGESTIONS FOR FURTHER READING

If you would like to read more about the first subway, here are some books I found enjoyable and useful. The best single book on Contract No. 1 is *The New York Subway: Its Construction and Equipment,* originally published in 1904 to celebrate the opening of the subway, but now available in a new edition (Bronx, N.Y.: Fordham University Press, 2004). It is packed with photographs, drawings, and detailed descriptions of subway construction, stations, the powerhouse and substations, tracks and signals, motors and cars, and how it all worked.

Looking at the beautiful photographs of the architecture, interiors, and workers operating the machinery in Christopher Payne's *New York's Forgotten Substations: The Power Behind the Subway* (New York: Princeton Architectural Press, 2002) is the next best thing to being inside a world very few people even know existed (a few of the original substations remained in operation over ninety years, until 1999). Since many of the machines have been dismantled and scrapped, this is the only way you will ever see them.

Brian J. Cudahy's *Under the Sidewalks of New York: The Story of the Greatest Subway System in the World* (Bronx, N.Y.: Fordham University Press, 1995) tells the story of how it all began and continues through nearly a century of subway history. Best of all is the author's account of his ride through fifteen miles of the subway with the motorman in his cab explaining everything along the way.

Library of Congress Cataloging-in-Publication Data
Weitzman, David.
   A subway for New York / David Weitzman.
     p. cm.
    ISBN-13: 978-0-374-37284-2
    ISBN-10: 0-374-37284-5
    1. Subways—New York (State)—New York—Juvenile literature. [1. Subways—New York (State)—New York.] I. Title.

TF847.N5W45 2005
625.4'2'097471—dc22

2004056286